In Imitation of Two Hearts

In Imitation of Two Hearts

Prayers for Consolation, Renewal and
Peace in Times of Suffering

Father John J. Pasquini

Copyright © 2006 John J. Pasquini

ISBN-10: 1-924222-20-8
ISBN-13: 978-1-934222-20-1

This book is printed in the United States.

Nihil Obstat:
   Rev. Dennis M. Duvelius
   Censor Librorum
   Archdiocese of Indianapolis

Imprimatur:
   Rev. Msgr. Joseph F. Schaedel
   Vicar General / Moderator of the Curia
   Archdiocese of Indianapolis

Cover Graphic Design: Mr. Philip Lobiondo
The cover design is a depiction of Jesus' grace showering His Mother from the heart, and in turn depicts Mary responding to this gift from her own heart.

Shepherds of Christ Publications
P.O. Box 627
China, Indiana 47250-0627

Tel: (812) 273-8405
Toll free: (888) 211-3041
Fax: (812) 273-3182
Email: info@sofc.org
http://www.sofc.org

Contents

Foreword: Dr. Carol J. Razza, Ed.D 9

Introduction 11

Chapter One: In Imitation of Jesus' Heart 13

Chapter Two: In Imitation of Mary's Heart 73

Chapter Three: Conclusion 91

To Renato and Florence Pasquini
parents who lived the mystery of suffering and love

Foreword

Dr. Carol Razza, M.S., Ed. D.

In my experience as a psychotherapist of nearly three decades, I have found one characteristic central to emotional, psychological, and physical healing: surrendering to God in prayer. Surrendering to God—the Creator and Supreme Being who knows our very design because he formed it--means giving oneself over to the one that can love us out of our suffering and into a peace that surpasses all human understanding.

There is no doubt in my mind that those individuals that embrace prayer in Jesus as they journey through their suffering come out on the other side of that suffering, healed, whole, and restored, in ways they never realized were possible. Prayer allows sufferers to shift their focus from suffering onto the truth that God can set them free.

The prayers in Father John Pasquini's book are inspired by God and based on that truth which can only bring the reader into a fuller relationship with Jesus and a closer relationship to the heart of his precious Mother.

Father John's book directs the hurting to a hope beyond hope, a hope which allows them to see beyond their suffering into the very truth of their existence as beings loved by God. When people surrender to God, God becomes their very focus and the eyes of their understanding are opened to embrace the reality of the God that has a plan for their lives—and God's plan stretches beyond this very moment in time: "For I know well the plans I have in mind for you, says the Lord, plans for your welfare, not for woe! Plans to give you a future full of hope" (Jer. 29:11).

Father Pasquini's book is about nurturing relationships with Jesus and Mary. As you pray through his book, embrace the hands of Jesus and Mary, and find the strength that comes from their companionship and love. God bless you on your journey.

Dr. Carol J. Razza *is a psychotherapist licensed by the state of Florida in mental health counseling. Her degrees include an Ed. D. in child and youth studies from Nova Southeastern University, an M.S. in counseling psychology from Nova Southeastern University and a B.S. in psychology from Florida Atlantic University.*

Dr. Razza is an author, fulltime faculty member, and formation advisor at St. Vincent de Paul Regional Seminary. She has worked in private practice as a psychotherapist for over twenty - five years. Carol is also a nationally and internationally recognized speaker at seminars, conferences, workshops, and retreats.

Introduction

"Suffering is a part of the mystery of being human."
His Holiness Pope John Paul II

There are two realities we deal with every day of our lives. On the one hand we desire a life of happiness, a life of peace and contentment, and on the other hand we recognize that life comes with suffering. How do we reconcile these two realities?

As people of God we believe that God reconciles these two realities; that in God, the Reconciler, the Savior, the Sanctifier, we can have a taste of happiness, a taste of peace and contentment, even amidst a life that inevitably and unavoidably comes with suffering, with trials and tribulations.

In our prayer to the Father, through the Son, and in the Spirit, and through the intercessory power of Mary, may we come to light, happiness, and peace.

May we embrace, in our times of difficulty, the words of the Scriptures: "I rejoice in my sufferings for your sake, and in my flesh I am filling up what is wanting in the afflictions of Christ on behalf of his body..." (cf. Col. 1:24). Let us embrace our mission of cooperating in the redemptive work of our Savior.

These prayers are intended for those who are experiencing moments of suffering. It is an ideal prayer book for those who are homebound, or in hospitals, rehabilitation facilities, nursing homes, or hospice. It is an ideal prayer book for those who have experienced a loss of some kind, whether of a job or a loved one.

To allow unavoidable suffering to simmer is destructive. To take the unavoidable and allow the grace of God to transform it is at the heart of the mystery of Christian healing.

May God grant those who pray these prayers the grace to find peace and a more profound love of God and neighbor amidst their difficulties.

I

In Imitation of Jesus' Heart

"Our Redeemer has sanctified pain and by so doing has given the Christian a right way of facing it. For us, pain does not come to hurt and destroy, but to raise to the heights."

Blessed Placid Riccardi

Paschal Journey

Dear Lord,
everyday my life mirrors the mystery which is You.
I laugh, I cry, I rejoice, I suffer.
And at night I slumber, I sleep, I die to the day,
only to awake, to be resurrected, into a new experience.
O Lord, may I always recognize the pattern of Your life in
my life and may I always seek to pattern my life after Yours.

Prayer

O God, to pray to You is to experience the fruits of joy,
the ascent of my being,
the surge of my heart,
a look toward heaven,
a cry for recognition and love,
an embrace of life.

Prayer as Gift

O Jesus, raise my mind and heart to the Father.
Grant me the gifts of humility and a contrite heart so as
to recognize that without You I can do nothing.
O Jesus, may my faith be authentic;
May it find its authenticity in prayer.

Jesus, Teach Me to Pray

O Jesus, Splendor of the Father, pray for me, in me, and
with me.
O Jesus, Brightness of Eternal Light, pray for me as my
Priest, my Head, and my God.
Teach me to convert my heart,
to seek reconciliation,
to love my enemies,
to pray for my persecutors,
to be attentive,
to be pure,
And to seek the kingdom.
O Jesus, Teacher of Teachers, teach me to struggle, to be
patient, and to persevere.
Lead me, O Lord, to pray in faith,
to seek and knock,
for You are the door and the way.
O Jesus, Breastplate of Hope, help me to recognize that all
things are possible to those who believe.
Embody in me a heart to do Your will.
O Jesus, Joy of Angels, teach me to pray.

Good Morning, Lord

Good morning, Lord.

I do not know what today will bring,

but help me to be prepared for the adventure.

I pray that You bless me, prompt me, and help me follow Your call.

In the difficulties of today comfort me.

In the joys of today help me rejoice.

In the anxieties and frustrations and fears give me the courage to go on.

In my successes and in my failures, make me realize

that You are there to mold and fashion me.

Help me, Lord, to recognize that life is an adventure with great safety and great dangers.

Wherever You lead me today, give me the strength

to embark on this adventure which You have prepared for me.

Unavoidable Suffering

O Lord, Refuge of the Sorrowful, what am I to do with unavoidable suffering?

I can suffer with You or I can suffer without You.

When I suffer without You, my suffering is unbearable.

When I suffer with and in You, my suffering is not only bearable but transforming and redemptive.

O Lord, Refuge of the Sorrowful, what am I to do with unavoidable suffering?

"Never waste it!"

Sharing in Your Redemptive Power

O Lord, You said to us through the apostle Paul:

"I rejoice in my sufferings for your sake, and in my flesh I am filling up what is lacking in the afflictions of Christ on behalf of his body, which is the Church...."

Let me not, O Lord, waste the unavoidable sufferings of life.

Help me to transform my sufferings so that they may be united to Your sufferings on the Cross.

Help me join You, O Lord, in the work of sanctification and salvation.

O Lord, grant me the grace to share in Your redemptive work.

Why me?

O Lord, help me to recognize that all things are a part of Your divine providence;

That somehow, perhaps in ways that I will never be able to understand on this earthly journey, all is for a purpose, for my salvation and the building up of Your kingdom.

May I realize that my anger, resentment, and even rage that I direct toward others in times of difficulty are simply expressions of fear.

Grant me the grace to recognize in my complaints and demands, whether internally or externally, there is a cry to be respected and understood, a cry to be seen as valuable.

Help me understand that in my grief and tears that I need others and I need God.

Help me to surrender and trust You, O Lord, and to accept the good advice of those entrusted with my care with humility, appreciation and patience.

Anxiety

O Precious Jesus, calm the anxieties of life.

Prevent me from being overly worried.

O Precious Jesus, grant me the gift of understanding and the humility to discover the conscious and subconscious sources of my anxieties and worries.

Grant me the gift of counsel so as to recognize my need for help,

the gift of courage to seek changes that foster spiritual and physical integration,

the gift of temperance so that I may moderate my irrational thoughts and feelings,

the gift of wisdom, knowledge and piety to calm my concerns in acts of prayer and spiritual exercises,

the gifts of hope, wisdom, knowledge and understanding to bring about the peace I so much desire and the recognition that all is in Your providential hands.

No Remnants

O Lord, aid me to never offer You the remnants of my life.

May I never waste the years of my youth, my sharp mind, my heart's affection, my powers and talents to be used for some future time.

May I know my time is now!

But if I have squandered my youth, grant me the grace to make the future a fruitful gift of love to You.

Grant me the gift of knowing that now is the time to serve You for tomorrow may never come!

Fragrance of Christ

O Lord, bless me with the gift of being a good example in word and deed,

for my words validate my deeds and my deeds validate my words.

May no one doubt who I am! A follower of Christ!

May my words and actions lead the weak to strength and the proud to humility.

Grant me, within my difficulties, the grace of a life

dedicated to dispersing the fragrance of Christ to all the world.

Emptying Myself

O Lord, grant me the grace to empty myself of all that is not for Your honor and glory.

As You, in the Incarnation, emptied Yourself of all,

except of that knowledge which was necessary for my salvation.

May I empty myself of all so that all I possess will be that which is necessary for my salvation.

As You, O Precious One, offered Yourself for the salvation of others, may I too be empowered by Your grace to offer myself for the salvation of others.

Help me to prove my true love for You in bearing life's trials and tribulations with patience and confidence, and with the appreciation of its value for me and others.

As God has no limits on his love for us may we have no limits on our love for Him.

As He has done so much for me, may I be willing to do as much for Him.

In His infinite goodness to me, may I seek to be infinitely good to Him.

As Jesus submitted His heart to the Father, may I submit my heart as willingly.

If all is a gift from Him, prevent me from being stingy with these gifts given to me in stewardship.

Lord Jesus

In my sadness, my tears and sighs, grant me submissive peace, the peace of knowing that all is a part of Your divine plan, that nothing is by chance or coincidence.

My spirit rebels, my soul complains, but may my heart embrace.

I walk in darkness, but with Your assurance I know that I will never be deserted or led astray.

I cast all my concerns on You because You will never let me down.

You are my stronghold in times of oppression and afflictions.

Whether as conqueror or eternal victim, "Thy will be done."

Your Way

O Lord, may I realize that when things are not going my way, that the world is a temporary pilgrimage in terms of my eternal destiny.

Help me, O Lord, to recognize that perfect peace and security lies in You alone.

When life is beyond my control, grant me the gift of

recognizing the need for humility and the need to rid myself of pride.

O Lord, You know my innermost being, better than I,
and therefore I entrust my life into Your hands.

May I, O Lord, find Your consolation in my need for You.

Sacred Heart of Jesus

O Sacred Heart, continue to show me Your infinite love.

At the Last Supper, John reclined upon Your heart.

At the foot of the Cross Your heart was pierced for my sins.

From the side of Your heart, blood and water flowed out,
signifying the gifts of Baptism and Eucharist.

Grant me, O Lord, a love like that of David's.

Make me a person that chases after Your heart.

Make me love the image and likeness of You and Your heart in the image and likeness of my neighbors.

O Sacred Heart, transform my hardened heart into a sacred heart.

O Sacred Heart of Jesus, may Your heart speak to my heart.

Sacred, Purifying Heart of Love

O Lord Jesus, You purify the hearts of all who love You.

Use this time of suffering as a means of prioritizing my life.

Help me to be nothing, so that I may be everything.

Help me to be detached of all, so that I may love all as You love all.

O Lord Jesus, You purify the hearts of all who love You.

I love You! Purify my heart!

A Walk into Mystery

I have died many deaths on this earthly walk.

I have given all that I could until I could give no more.

I have cried out, "My God, my God, why have You forsaken me?"

Why has life dealt me such a blow?

I have no more to give.

I surrender and trust.

O Lord, Refuge of the Sorrowful, I walk into the unknown, into Your mystery.

Love of the Cross

Many love Jesus' heavenly kingdom,
but few love his Cross.
Many love rejoicing in Him
but few will suffer for Him.
Many love consolations
but few love His trials and tribulations.
Many love being at the table of the Lord
but few love His fasts and the bitter cup of His passion.
Many seek miracles
but hide their eyes from the Cross.
Many follow Him in good times
but quickly leave Him in times of difficulty.
O Lord, teach me to love You out of pure love
and without self-interest or self-infatuation.
Make me a lover of You, Lord, and not of self.
Make me poor in spirit with a heart
directed to Your honor and glory and my eternal destiny.

Purpose and Meaning

What attracts me to You, O God?

Is it purpose and meaning?

Am I more than a complex organism that is born, lives, struggles, and dies in emptiness?

Is life but a farce?

Is there more than mere existence, mere survival?

O God, You give me purpose and meaning.

You make life significant and of value!

O Infinite Being, continue to be my light, my way, my truth.

Providence

In the past I have done what I wanted and have found so much emptiness.

Now I recognize that a life lived without Your consultation is a life with disastrous outcomes.

Bless me, O Lord, in prioritizing my life so that all may flow from You and be returned to You as a blessing and a gift.

Help me, O Lord, to never abandon Your providential care for me.

Teach me the way You want me to live my life.

Seek

Ask and you will receive, seek and you will find.

Help me to realize that Your love for me is so great that You will never grow weary of my prayers, that You will always answer my prayers in such a way that I may give glory to You and acquire the gift of salvation.

You, O Lord, grant that which is always best for my sanctification and salvation.

Simplicity of Heart

Bless me with a simplicity of heart.

Speak to my heart so that my heart can speak to Yours.

May the words of grace that flow through Your heart touch my heart.

May my very being be penetrated with Your presence.

If I have found You nothing can disturb me,

for You are the victory, the triumph, the success of my life.

Divided Heart

O Lord, You have made me for You.

Bless me with a heart that is not divided, but completely absorbed in loving You.

Bless me with a small part of Your Mother's Sacred Heart, so that I may never be divided in my thoughts, will, and actions.

May I realize that my heart will never rest until it rests in You.

Take away my lukewarmness, my coldness, my sinfulness, my lack of fidelity.

Take away my fear of the future and replace it with the assurance of Your loving providence.
O Lord, You have made me for You.
Grant me a simple heart, a heart similar to Your Mother's, a heart that rests in Your heart.

Grace, My Teacher

Grace does not do away with life's trials and tribulations,
but it does help us to bear them in a fruitful manner.
Grace transforms disasters into gifts,
loss into gain,
darkness into light,
vice into virtue,
and death into life.
O precious grace, O precious Jesus,
You may not do away with life's trials and tribulations
but You do help me to bear them and transform them.

Foot of the Cross

O precious Lord, aid me in finding comfort in my sorrows.
Grant me the gift of strength and courage.
When I feel afflicted, bitter, abandoned, lonely, scorned,
buffet me with consolation.
When I am inflicted by darkness and misfortune,
grant me redemption and hope.
While the earth may shake, the heavens darken,
You are there to be my comfort.

Forgive them Father

Forgive them Father, for they know not what they do!

Amidst the curses, the injuries, the persecutions,

forgive them for they know not what they do.

Amidst the pain, the anguish, the distress, the misery,

the agony, the torment, and the afflictions,

forgive them for they know not what they do.

Amidst the indignant, the disagreeable, the resentful, the displeased, the suspicious,

forgive them for they know not what they do.

Amidst the dissatisfied, the jealous, the prideful, the intolerant, the distrustful,

forgive them for they know not what they do.

Amidst the vengeful, the bitter, the unfriendly, the stubborn, the uncooperative,

forgive them for they know not what they do.

Amidst the loathful, the critical, the annoyed, the irritated,

forgive them for they know not what they do.

Amidst the antagonistic, the hostile, the outraged, the quarrelsome, the impatient,

forgive them for they know not what they do.

Amidst the defiant, the sarcastic, the disobedient, the rebellious, the demanding, the greedy,

forgive them for they know not what they do.

O Lord, may I live in Your love, by Your love, and for Your love so that I may know the meaning and the gift of forgiveness.

May my last words on this earthly journey be:

"Forgive them Father, for they know not what they do."

No, Not Me!

Lord, help me to get over the shock and panic of my suffering.

Move me from "it can't be true" to acceptance, from "there must be a mix up" to a reassurance that all will be fine.

Buffer me, O Lord, from my fears and tears.

Infuse me with the ability to collect and mobilize myself so as to deal with the unexpected, the unknown.

Shatter my defenses and help me to face my difficulties.

May I face today what cannot be postponed for tomorrow.

Help me to talk about my concerns and to accept what needs to be done.

Isolation

O Lord, help me to fight the temptation to isolate myself.

Grant me the gift to never walk alone in this valley of tears.

May my friends not abandon me out of fear, but understand me and support me.

May they and I realize the need to be needed, the need to not be left alone.

May my true friends come to light and become light in my time of isolation and darkness.

May You, and Your precious Mother, be my companions along the journey.

Nourish me with friends, heavenly and earthly.

Getting Through Dark Nights

O Jesus, when the clouds of darkness fall upon me grant me the gifts to persevere in patience, trust, and humility.

Grant me the gift to keep my eyes focused on You and Your Cross,

the gift of a docile spirit where I am open, despite my difficulties and discomforts,

to follow You with the understanding that You are the God who controls history,

that You are the God who in Your providence will make all things "alright."

Grant me a will so empowered with faith that I may conquer the difficulties and darknesses of life.

Climbing Calvary

Lord Jesus, help me to carry my cross with You and for You.

O Lord, help me to climb upon the Cross and share in Your glory,

to unite my sufferings with Yours,

my flowing tears to Your flowing blood,

my climb upon my own cross with Your climb,

my suffering with Your suffering and work of redemption.

Just as You suffer for me, with me and in me,

may I suffer in You, for You, and with You.

Grant me, O Lord, the courage and grace to embrace the crosses of life with a spirit of victory.

Crushed to the Ground

O Lord, I often feel as if I have been crushed into the ground.

I feel the pain of the fall every time that I am lonely, depressed, or ill.

I feel the sting of the ground every time I struggle to pray.

I feel the tearing of my knees every time darkness seems to hide my faith and hope.

O Lord, grant me the grace to imitate You in continually rising from the ground.

Help me to recognize that this suffering is but a momentary experience within the scope of eternity.

What do You ask of Me?

O Lord, what do You ask of me?

Confidence, my child!

Surrender and Trust!

Surrender and trust through times of suffering,

through times of pain,

of anguish,

of distress,

of misery,

of agony,

of torment,

of affliction,

of doubt,

of agitation

of disturbances

of anxieties,

of abandonment,

of loneliness,

of injustices,

of a damaged reputation.

Grant me, O Lord, confidence in Your providence.

Mold me in Your image and likeness.

Grant me the spirit of the spouse of the Holy Spirit, Mary.

O Lord, what do You ask of me?
Confidence, my child.
Surrender and Trust.

You are there!

You are there, O God, when I dare to pray into silent darkness,

when I walk into the unknown unconditionally,

when I fall and learn of Your mercy, forgiveness, and power of renewal,

when desperation is accepted and trust in You is made more precious,

when I recognize my pending death and find peace and composure.

You are there, O God, even when I do not know it.

You are there, O God, to make every day a walk into the mystical.

You are there…

From Darkness into Light

O Lord, lead me from darkness into Your light.

It is in the ordinary and extraordinary facets of life

that You make me into what You want me to be.

It is through the ordinary and extraordinary illnesses, bereavements, estrangements, separations, misunderstandings, struggles, and all forms of failure that You, O Lord, can change every fiber of my being.

May I never lose sight of or fear this reality!

Nothing is coincidence!

Nothing is chance!

Blind me not!

Awaken the light!

May I see the Providence!

May I see through the darkness into this most precious of lights.

May I accept Your love, endure with patience the darkness, and open my eyes in humility to the light of my happiness and salvation.

May I emerge from this crucible brighter and purer than fire tried gold.

Always There

Jesus, You were there for me in the past.

Aid me, now, to recognize that You are here for me now, and will be forever more.

I have seen Your power, Your goodness, Your fidelity, Your understanding of my needs, weaknesses, and powerlessness.

I have seen Your miracles in my life.

You were there in all Your glory in the past;

Why should I doubt Your presence in the present and the future?

O Jesus, just as You were there for me in the past, I know you will be with me now and forever more.

Stages

Heavenly Savior, purge me so that I may grow to love You with my whole heart.

Illuminate me so that I may love You with my whole soul.

Unite me to You so that I may become complete.

Heavenly Savior, grant me the gift of being purged, illuminated, and united to You.

In Me, with Me, and for Me

O Lord, may I always be conscious of Your presence.

May I always recognize that you are living in me, always present to me, always working for my good by moving and governing my entire being within the gift of freedom.

You are always there to embrace me, sustain me, and enlighten me.

O Lord, may I always be conscious of Your presence.

Teach Me How to Suffer

O Lord, teach me how to suffer with simplicity;

Without useless self-absorption;

In total abandonment to Your Will.

Grant me the grace to deal with my difficulties in a spirit of calm, serenity, and courage from day to day and from moment to moment.

Take away my tendency to worry about tomorrow.

Take away my tendency to exaggerate, ponder, foster, obsess and nurture an unhealthy preoccupation over these difficulties;

And most especially, take away any hindrance within my suffering that makes me insensible and indifferent to the suffering of others.

Aid me, O Lord, to go beyond myself to others and to meet their needs as I wish my needs to be met;

Help me to alleviate the hardships of others as I wish mine

to be alleviated.

Bless me with the grace to bear my crosses
and to recognize that I am never alone in this journey!

O Infant Jesus

O Infant Jesus, grant me a spirit of poverty.

You laid in a manger.

You traveled so often without a place to lay Your precious head.

And when You aged, You finally rested on the Cross.

In my time of difficulty, grant me a spirit of poverty.

Help me to be detached of all so that I may love all as You love all!

O Infant Jesus, make me realize that if I have You, I have everything!

Drowned

O Lord, may I never be exasperated and drowned in my sorrow.

May I always have the grace to see beyond myself and maintain my charity, my generosity, my balance, and my worship of You, O Lord.

May I magnanimously overcome myself and see my sufferings as means to holiness.

When things seem lost, when things seem to be over my head, when I seem to be drowning with no hope in sight, grant me the grace and trust to take a walk of faith into the mystery of the unknown, into Your embracing arms and Your will;

May You be my refuge in these times;

May You be a light in this darkness.

Internal Changes

In You, O Lord, my external situation may not change, but my internal being shall;

If only I can abandon my fears and trust, You will console me, sustain me, and grant me the gift of perseverance.

If only I can cast my cares upon You, O Lord, upon Your providence, upon Your divine plan for me, then all things will be just fine.

May I realize that all, absolutely all, is in Your hands!

Bless me with trust!

Mystery of the Cross

Help me, O Lord, to penetrate the mystery of all mysteries.

Aid me in understanding that within the mystery of suffering is the mystery of love and that within the mystery of love is the mystery of suffering.

May I see this by the supernatural light of faith!

May I see my troubles not as instruments of despair but as means of purification, expiation, sanctification, and ultimate union with You, my God.

Through these sufferings enlarge the powers of my soul beyond a contentment for mediocrity and into the privileged place of so few,

divine union with You my Creator and Hope.

Grant me the grace to embrace my heart's deepest desires, that which is completely for Your honor and glory.

Supreme Love

Lord Jesus, in Your Cross You showed Your supreme love for me.

In my small cross, grant me the grace to show my supreme love for You.

May the instrument of death, the Cross, be an instrument of mutual love, a reflection of my love for You and Your love for me.

May I unite my little crosses to Your great Cross.

Denial

O Lord, when I am unable to face my sufferings, wake me up from my denial.

Grant me the grace of not being concerned with whether my life is being interfered with as much as how my life is being lived with all fullness and authenticity.

Support me in recognizing my mortality, not as something to be feared, but as a gift that sets my priorities straight.

Where there is denial in my life, may You bring me to the point of acceptance and peace, to the point of faith and trust.

Worry

O Lord, may I not be overcome with what I cannot control.

May I not obsess about tomorrow, about my finances, my job, my change in life, my dependence on others, my insecurity.

Bless me with the gift to apprehend that all is a part of Your divine providence, that nothing is by chance, that all is for Your honor and glory—even when it is beyond my comprehension to grasp.

Grant me the grace to never forget I am a crucial part of life and a crucial part in Your redemptive work.

Soften My Heart

O Divine Lord, soften my heart so I may experience you.

Help me to conquer my psychological fears, flaws, and unresolved issues and seek that which is beyond my comfort level.

O Divine Lord, take away my fear, soften my heart, and help me to realize my true identity in Your presence.

Support me in acknowledging that I am the only act of creation that You willed for its own sake.

Understood

Grant me the gift of being understood and empathized with when I am sad.

Grace me with the need to face what needs to be faced and not fall into the trap of delusion.

I am sad, may it be acknowledged and empathized with.

I am lonely,

I am bitter,

I am sorrowful,

I am grief-stricken,

I am confused,

I am disappointed, displeased

I am resentful,

I am distrustful,

I am indignant,
I am irritated,
I am depressed; may it be acknowledged and empathized with.
Teach me to own my feelings, to make them truly mine.
Just sit near me and be with me.
Stroke my hair, hold my hand, caress my tears.
Grant me the grace to look forward.

Resting in God

Only in You, Lord, will I find rest.
I desired happiness, yet recognized that life comes with suffering?
I searched high and low for meaning and purpose.
I sought it in power, and found it fleeting, disappointing, poisonous and empty.
I sought fame, and found it paralyzing and self-absorbing.
I sought fortune, and found it addictive and never enough.
****
I chased and chased and chased till I could no longer chase.
I was conquered.
And in this conquest, I was given victory;
for in You I found my peace.
Amidst hatred, You gave me the gift of forgiveness.
Amidst injury, You gave me patience.
Amidst doubt, You gave me insight.
Amidst sadness, You gave me hope.
Amidst depression, You gave me consolation.
Amidst greed, You gave me generosity.
Amidst apathy, You gave me empathy.
Amidst all of life's trials and tribulations, You give me that

taste of happiness, peace, and contentment that finds its ultimate fulfillment in heaven.

Only in You, O Lord, do I find rest.

Failures

O Lord, grant me the grace to accept the failures and lost opportunities of the past.

Grant me the humility to accept that I am no longer the provider, but the one that needs to be provided for.

May my sorrows and grief be moments of freedom and detachment in order to receive the gift of Your peace.

Grace me with the gift of working through my anguish and anxiety, of fulfilling my capacity to accomplish Your will— even when Your will is difficult to perceive.

Numb

I feel weak, numb, thin.

My self-esteem has been damaged.

I cannot smile.

I am no longer what I was.

I feel overwhelmed with a sense of loss and depression.

My financial and physical burdens are overwhelming and dismaying.

I miss my children, my spouse, my life as it was.

What does the future hold?

Will I see my old age?

Will my job be there for me?

Are all my future dreams a thing of the past?

What will happen to my family?

What has my suffering brought upon others?

May I see my difficulties as a means of appreciating the truly important things of life.

New Role

Grace me with the comfort of a new role in life.

May I now empty myself of the need to attend to the needs of others;

Rather grant me the meekness and humility to accept from others what I have always given to others, love.

I have a new role now.

Grace me with the comfort of this new role in life.

My Ultimate Goal

O Divine Savior, make me realize that my rest and happiness depends on You as my ultimate goal, that all is to be done for Your honor and glory, that the only thing that counts and the only thing which my life should be directed towards is my eternal destiny.

O Lord, make me realize that my rest and happiness depends on You as my ultimate goal.

Dignity

O Lord, may I never lose my dignity.

Bless me with being understood, not judged,

with being accepted, not rejected.

May my being different not be feared, but embraced.

Help me to accept that despite my difference I am still loved.

May my pain not be ignored but acknowledged and empathized with.

Tired

When I am so tired that I could cry, send me others to reinvigorate me.

When the pain is too much to handle, grant me grace to endure it.

When I am too tired to pray, grant me Your Holy Spirit to pray for me and in me.

Facing the Difficult

Grant me the courage to face reality,

to not postpone the inevitable,

but to accept my unique journey.

May I be childlike and wide-eyed in accepting my circumstances.

Take away from me the temptation to bargain my way out of my troubles.

May I accept my situation, recognize God's providence,

and surrender and trust that all will be just fine.

May I realize that I was created for "eternity."

Wounds of the Battle

The wounds of the battle help me to see where I am on the road to You.

By observing my wounds I know how close I am to victory
or defeat—how much I have become vigilant and how
much I have become lax.

My distractions help me to see what I am attached to and
who is my master.

My dryness is a reminder to walk in faith or repent and turn
back to You.

My seemingly unanswered prayers help to clarify
my motives:

Do I love You as an instrument of selfishness

or as a God who deserves love for simply being God?

Do I wait to see how You answer my prayers in ways that
are best for my eternal destiny?

O God, pray in me, for me, and with me.

O God, bless me with the gift of humility and trust

and thus empower me to persevere in the battle.

Victory leads to enlightenment, peace and happiness.

Defeat leads to slavery.

O God, grant me victory.

Postpone Not!

Let me not postpone for tomorrow what can be done today.
Help me to recover so as to fulfill my divine mission,
a mission dedicated to the building up of the kingdom,
of service to the Church,
of loving God and neighbor.
May my worries, my guilt, my emotions not overcome me;
Rather may they be a source of renewal.
Let me not postpone for tomorrow what can be done today.

Seeing Dimly

I see dimly now as in a mirror.

I await the day when I will see You as You are.

On that day I will experience what eye has never seen, nor ear has ever heard.

On that day I will see what You have prepared for those who love You.

I see dimly now as in a mirror.

I await the day when I will see You as You are.

Penetrating the Depths of the Cross

In my unavoidable suffering, help me to enter into the thicket of the Cross.

In abandonment and desolation grant me supernatural faith, hope and love.

When I have been given a Judas kiss and been berated by the "high priests" and "secular soldiers" of the world, grant me consolation in Your unconquerable will.

When my closest friends have abandoned me and said, "I do not know the man," grant me the gift of forgiveness.

In being scourged, spat upon, blindfolded, and crowned with thorns, grant me the grace to return hatred with love.

When I cry "let this chalice pass from me," let me respond with "not as I will, but as You will."

When the cross seems too heavy for me to carry on and the crowds yell, "crucify him, crucify him," grant me the grace to persevere till the end.

In this rapid crescendo of torture, may I never lose sight of You, my Lord, my comfort, my consolation, my victory.

If all the world were to desert me, You, O Lord, would be here!

In trustful abandonment, in complete submission to Your will, and in the fatigued words, "into Thy hands I commend my spirit," may I find Your Resurrection, Your Victory, Your Conquest!

Hope against All Hope

O Lord, source of invincible hope, teach me to hope against all hope.

Where there is obscurity, grant me firmness of faith.

Where there is adversity and a sense of abandonment, bless me with perseverance.

Where there is darkness and doubt, grant me the ability to make a meritorious act of faith.

Where there is a crucible of trials, bless me with the gift of having my very being purified as gold in a furnace.

Where there is suffering of mind and body, where there is the void of abandonment and helplessness, where there is distrust, confusion, discouragement, and even despair, grant me the gift of willing myself through these realities and to You.

May I always be blessed with the understanding that, in grace, I will never be pushed beyond my capacity to deal with my difficulties nor shall You, O Lord, ever abandon me unless I abandon You!

When I do not *feel* hope, make me *will* hope!

Take care, Lord

Take care of me Lord when I weep at night.

Tend to me in my suffering.

Grant me rest when I am weary.

Bless me when I need soothing from my suffering.

Take care of me Lord when I weep at night.

Overwhelmed

I put all in Your hands, O Lord.

I trust You as I walk into the unknown.

I will do all that is possible, and within my grasp, to accept the often overwhelming.

I recognize that You have a plan for me.

I accept all that is necessary.

I trust that Your desire for me will be fulfilled, perhaps in ways I will never truly know.

I put all in Your hands, O Lord.

Depending

I have always been self-sufficient.

Grant me the grace to surrender and trust.

Let me put my dependence on You, O Lord,

and on those You have entrusted with my care.

Grant me the humility to accept being loved.

Listen to Me

May I be listened to and not left alone.

Grant me reassurance as people observe my look, my hand pressure, my leaning back into my pillow, my sigh, my grimace.

May they understand, O Lord, my need for detachment at times and my need for attachment at others.

May they "hold on" when I need to be held onto and may they "let go" when I am ready to let go.

Bless me, O Lord, with spiritually eared people!

My Miseries

O Christ, forgive me of my complaints in times of suffering, for I have not so suffered to the point of shedding my blood like that of the martyrs.

My little miseries are nothing when compared to those who underwent strong and violent temptations and tests.

O Christ, forgive me of my complaints in times of suffering.

Teach me to bear my little miseries patiently, willingly, and without complaint, that nothing that I can suffer goes without merit!

Without the battle, there is no victory, there is no crown!

Courage and Patience

Teach me, O Lord, to bear the unavoidable sufferings of life with courage and patience.

In times of unpleasantness, ailments, exhaustion, separation, loneliness, intemperance, aridity, weariness, temptations, change, struggle, storms, opposition, contradictions, dangers, privations, pains and persecutions, teach me to endure, surmount, and overcome what I encounter.

Grant me, O Lord, the courage and patience to bear all in a spirit of serenity for love of You.

Support me in transforming these crosses into sources of purification, sources for molding my entire being into what You want me to be.

May You transform these sufferings into a means of accepting Your Love and heavenly will, of growing in the virtues, and of receiving the gift of union and intimacy with You.

Help me, O Lord, to accept my sufferings in conformity to Your will.

A Savior's Love

O God, You chastise me with Your loving power.

When I lack faith, You show me how to experience the emptiness of a life without You.

When I lack hope, You show me glimpses of despair.

When I lack love, You show me loneliness.

When I lack prudence, You show me the hurt I cause to others.

When I lack patience, You show me reminders that I am not in control.

When I lack temperance, You show me that a life that is out of control is a life not worth living.

When I lack modesty, You show my ugliness.

When I lack kindness, You show me the sting of those who hate me.

When I lack courage, You show me that I have but one life to live.

When I lack perseverance, You show me the kind of strength that is needed to keep on going.

When I forget You, You show me the hard ache of tribulation to set my priorities straight, to reorient my eyes toward You.

O God, in Your love You always want my happiness.

O God, in Your love You are always there to put me on the right track.

O God, You chastise me with Your loving power.

O God, You are my loving Savior.

Eternal Hope

O Lord of hope, You give me strength in suffering.

You prolong my spirit till I can understand and accept

my condition.

You make a nightmare, a sweet dream,

despair into a promising future, a promising end.

You take away my insignificant fears and give me purpose and meaning.

You maintain my spirit and nourish me in times of need.

You give me confidence and appreciation amidst the bad news.

Bless me with the recognition that the ultimate miracle is peace, acceptance, and confidence in You.

May I always remember that I am a child of eternal hope.

Walking into Acceptance

Walk me, O Lord, through my depression, my anger, and my envy for the healthy and well-off.

Sustain me in mourning my losses, whether of family, friends, places or things.

May I quietly expect and accept Your divine providence.

I am now void of feelings.

The final stage before the long journey begins.

The fight is over; victory awaits.

Grant me, O Lord, the gift to embrace the peace and dignity that is before me.

Walk with me!

To become Anew

O Precious Spirit, grant me the gifts to become now what I would want to be at the end of my life.

Grace me with a perfect contempt of the world, an ardent desire for the virtuous life, and a love of discipline.

Bless me with perseverance in prayer, the gifts of faith, hope and love, the gifts of chastity, obedience, and poverty in spirit.

Grant me a desire for the denial of self and the gift of patiently bearing the attacks of my enemies with confidence and assurance of victory.

O Precious Lord, grant me the gifts to become now what I would want to be at the end of my life.

Into the Mystery

O Mystery of Mysteries, may I journey into You.

O Mystery of Mysteries, grant me the gift to move forward in the spiritual life.

Purify me, illuminate me, and unite me to You.

Grant me the courage to move into the unknown where You are in Your fullness.

Take away my fear and my predisposition for retreating into what is comfortable and asks no faith of me.

Lord Jesus, may I journey into the unknown, into the mystery which is You.

In the Garden

Not my will but Thy will be done!

Teach me, O Lord, to express my denials, my anger, and even my rage.

Teach me, O Lord, to express my fears, my grief, my attempts at bargaining, my fantasies of what could have been.

Help me to find and accept what You, O Lord, have planned for me from all eternity.

Sustain me in the knowledge that there are no coincidences

and no chance occurrences.
Bless me with the sense of providence.
Not my will but Thy will be done!

Mortification

Christ has many who desire Him, but few who will sacrifice for Him.

The tears of life cleanse the soul but the lack of tears extinguish its light.

O Jesus, Fount of Eternal Wisdom, may my passions be in order with right reason and the proper use of my will. May they lead me away from self-destruction and slavery.

O Jesus, our Way and our Life, may I seek to be attached to all that is for Your honor and glory and become detached of all that is not for Your honor and glory.

O Jesus, our Refuge, may I seek to empty myself of all but You.

O Jesus of Great Counsel, may I have the strength to deny my passions and appetites in order to purify them and in order to purify my path to You.

O Jesus, Treasure of the Faithful, may I grow in detachment, mortification, obedience, self-discipline and simplicity.

O Jesus, Seat of Eternal Wisdom, may I be aware of deceptive and inordinate pleasures which are momentary, but in the long run lead to sadness and remorse.

O Jesus, meek and humble of heart, make me indifferent to all, so that I may love all. May I grow in self-mastery so that I may enter the heart of holiness and happiness.

O Jesus, Lover of Creation, may my passions be in order with right reason and the proper use of my will.

Christ has many who desire Him, but few who will sacrifice for Him.

The tears of life cleanse the soul but the lack of tears extinguishes its light.

Gratitude

Thank You, O Lord, for all You do is directed toward my salvation.

Thank You, O Lord, for hard work rather than rest,

for the cross rather than comfort,

for the dryness in prayer rather than consolation;

For in the cross is found my source of purification and salvation, and in the dryness I learn to love You for simply being You.

Thank you for relegating me to the lowest places, for in Your kingdom I will enjoy the most precious of places.

Thank You, God, for punishments, chastisements, and afflictions, for through them You teach me the value of humility, generosity, chastity, mildness, temperance, and diligence.

Thank You, O Lord, for all You do for me is directed toward my salvation.

Tasting Heaven

O Precious Lord, grant me the gift to act in accordance with the demands of faith, hope, and love.

Shower me with Your flares of grace, divine touches, words of love, and darts of compassion.

Shower me with Your self-communicating presence that enables me to act in a salutary, beneficial, curative, and holy manner.

Grant me that interior impulse, that attraction, that

illumination or interior light that is a taste of heaven.

Sustain me with strength, courage, endurance and those thoughts and feelings that arise only from You.

O Divine Savior, grant me a taste of heaven.

Hope in Failure

In all that I have done I have been a failure.

I accomplished little and produced even less.

I have left little behind.

My one comfort, O Compassionate One, is that You never called me to be successful, but only faithful.

Perhaps this, in the end, I will fulfill.

A Helping Hand

O Lord, grant me the grace to need You.

Grant me the grace to understand that You are my light and my salvation.

In my fragile state, with all its miseries, insufficiencies, weaknesses, failures, infidelities, and annoyances, bless me with confidence.

In my inappropriate attachments, bless me with an unshakable hope.

In my painful and arduous struggles and inner groans, bless me with a humble heart.

In my desire for humility and meekness, in my recognition of my imperfections, You are there stretching out Your hand to help me.

Hopeful

When I feel hopeless, O Lord, send me hope.

When there is an inability to understand,

when people "write me off" bless me with optimism.

When I am desperate, keep me from breaking.

When I am abandoned and deserted, hold my hand.

And when all earthly hope is exhausted, bathe me in supernatural hope.

Make everyday a miracle, a new lease on life, a comeback.

Words beyond Words

O Lord, may the unexplainable be accepted.

Teach my loved ones to not necessarily understand, but to accept.

Grant them the grace to accept my sighs, wet eyes, smiles, gestures of the hands, empty looks, astonished glances, and outstretched hands as words beyond words.

May they empathize with me in this mystery of words beyond words.

A Reed in the Wind

Where are all the famous people?

In their lifetime they enjoyed fame, worldly honors, and notoriety, but today they are scarcely remembered.

Their fame has been supplanted.

O how foolish to chase after that which is so short lived.

O holy and precious Lord bless me with the wisdom to chase after Your heart.

Grant me the wisdom to desire Your will and everlasting life with You.

Blessed Tears

Blessed are those who mourn, for they shall be comforted by the God who is our hope, our anchor, our only happiness.

Help me, O Lord, to shed tears which are pleasing to You and which lead me to You.

Help me to mourn over the time I wasted on vanities, self-infatuation, self-complacency, and the desire for the esteem of others.

May my tears clean my soul from sin and dispose my life for friendship with God.

May my tears help me to make profound examinations of conscience.

Grant me the ability to mourn so that my life may reflect true contrition.

Bless me with tears of sorrow and repentant love and not with tears of discouragement.

Blessed are those who mourn, for they shall be comforted by You, our hope, our anchor, our only happiness.

Through the Desolation

Where are You, O Lord?

Where is Your consolation?

Where are Your answers to my prayers?

Why the desolation?

***

My child, you are closer to me than you know!

Do not be anxious, dismayed or disturbed.

It is in these times that I ask you to love me for simply being me.

I have given you much in the past and so you loved me.

Now I withdraw all, so that you may be purified.

Love me for simply being me!

Your reward shall be great!

Chastised

I am happy to be chastised by You, O God, for You heal me as You wound me.

You blind me, God of Majesty, to help me see authentically;

You deafen me, so I can hear genuinely;

You make me mute, so I can speak Your words more eloquently;

You dull my senses so I can experience life faithfully.

I am happy to be chastised by You, O God, for You heal me as You wound me.

Sacred Heart

Sacred Heart of Jesus, wounded out of love for me, have mercy on me.

Sacred Heart of Jesus, grant me the grace to recognize my sins and the ability to make reparation for the wounds I have inflicted upon You by my sinfulness.

In my forgetfulness, indifference, pride, covetousness, lust, anger, gluttony, envy and sloth I pierce Your Sacred Heart.

Grant me the grace to overcome my blindness.

Grant me the gift of offering up my sufferings to expiate and repair in justice and love what I have failed to do.

Jesus You cry out, "My Heart seeks to be comforted?"

Let me cry out in response, "O Lord, may I be a comfort to Your Sacred Heart."

Healing of Memories

O Lord, release my memories.

Open the flood gates.

Bless me with the grace to work through my rational and irrational feelings.

Eliminate my evasiveness, my facades and make-believe masks.

Get me out of my negative emotional patterns and recurring cycles of destruction.

O Great Physician, heal the wounds that torment me, the abuse, the losses, the overwhelming mental and emotional pains.

Heal what time cannot heal.

Heal the sensitive spots, emotions, and traumas.

Soothe my damaged body, soul, and spirit.

Console me in Your healing arms.

Comfort

O Lord, help me to love what I ought to love, know what I ought to know, loathe what I ought to loathe, and ignore what I ought to ignore.

O Lord, when I am defiled by sins, be my comfort.

When I am enmeshed in disquietude and carnal thoughts,

when I am overwhelmed by doubts and fears,

when I am attacked by unceasing cares, curiosities and endless vanities, when I am blinded by errors, vexed by temptations, and torn down by the world's allurements, comfort me.

O Lord, be my comfort in my exile by giving me the strength to die to self so that you may be all in all.

When evil people prosper and my good intentions fail,

when others are listened to and I am ignored,

when others are accepted and I am refused,

when others are promoted and fondly thought of, and I am judged unfit, be my comfort.

O Lord, help me to love what I ought to love, know what I ought to know, loathe what I ought to loathe, and ignore what I ought to ignore.

Dryness

O Lord, Good Shepherd, help me in my times of dryness in prayer, in times when I experience a loss of consolation, peace, happiness, and comfort.

Sustain me in times when I feel that prayer is burdensome.

O Gentle Shepherd, may the dryness never overcome me;

May I never abandon the spiritual battle.

Make me realize that in this dryness You are closer than ever; that You are asking me to love You with a pure faith for simply being You, and not for the goods and consolations You give me.

May I remain faithful in this dryness so that I may exit it

a deeper and more profound person, a person of profound insight.

May I experience the newness of life that only You can give.

O Good Shepherd, lead me in such a way that I may always love You for simply being You.

Desire Nothing

Our God embraced poverty, privations, and hardships.
Should I not imitate Him?

In order to possess everything I must desire to possess nothing;

For it is in being detached of all that I can love the way You want me to love, purely.

To be free of all, is to be open to all and to love all that is for Your honor and glory.

Allow me to resolve and strip myself of everything that could hinder my union with You, particularly acts of self-infatuation, pride, vanity, and faulty pretensions.

May I shred myself, for love of You, of my desire for riches, material well-being, and superficial comforts.

In order to possess everything I must desire to possess nothing.

Sustain me with the grace to do all for Your honor and glory and to put away the old desires for my own honor and glory.

Support me with the grace to freely embrace life's journey in total freedom, in total authenticity.

Bless me with the gift to say, "Lord, I love You more than myself and above all things."

Awareness

O Lord, I am filled with regrets, insecurity, ambivalence, bewilderment, guilt, resentment, and even lack of independence.

I am overwhelmed by change, by a need to adapt and adjust.

Where is the balance in my life that once was there?

Where is the meaning and purpose in my life?

O Lord, help me to adjust to my new circumstances, new arrangements, new atmosphere.

Help me, O Lord of the Universe, to express what I am unable to express.

Grant me the courage to hear what I need to hear and not what I think I need to hear.

Grant me an awareness of my projection of feelings and emotions onto others.

Take away my fear of fulfilling expectations.

Gift me with the awareness of the value of life in and of itself and my place within Your divine plan.

Value of Christian Suffering

O Lord, bless me with the gift of understanding the mystery and value of suffering.

In a world that only sees prosperity, materialism, and earthly glory as valuable, the mystery of the Cross and spirituality is beyond the scope of understanding.

O Lord may this mystery not be a stumbling block or foolishness to me.

May I, however, see in the unavoidable sufferings of life a means to redemption and salvation.

Grant me, O Lord, the ability to unite my sufferings with Yours, to allow the unavoidable sorrows and pains of suffering to sanctify me and prepare me for eternity.

Take away my blindness, darkness, and uncertainty in regard to this mystery and grant me enlightenment.

Embracing the Cross

O Lord, help me to accept and embrace the crosses of life.
Life has not made me powerful, famous, wealthy, or attractive.
But life has given me what is most precious.
Life has given me You.
O Lord, help me to accept my crosses and learn to be what I have and who I am.

A Victim Offering

O Lord, help me take the unavoidable everyday ordinary sufferings in my life and offer myself up as a victim soul, a victim soul inspired by the spirit of atonement.
As a victim soul I seek to avoid sin, to patiently endure life's difficulties, and to have a heart that is entirely submissive to Your divine will.
Help me, O Lord, to be a victim of Your Sacred Heart.
Place me, O Divine Priest, on Your altar, and consume me, Your victim, by the fires of Your Sacred Heart.

Distractions

O Lord, may nothing ever take hold of my heart and impede my progress toward You.
May I never fear facing what needs to be faced.
Prevent me from stifling my sorrows with worldly infatuations, with distractions that blind me to my true self.
Grant me the grace to see when I am running away
from problems, as opposed to confronting them.

Grace me with the gift of conquering those desires that are warring against my soul.

May I never endanger, delay, or be detained from my pilgrimage.

May I never fail to fight the good fight, to win the race.

Grant me the gift to forget the emptiness of "earthly things" with a detached heart and a love for heavenly things.

O Lord, may nothing ever take hold of my heart and impede my progress toward You.

Trials and Tribulations

You cannot flee trials, tribulations and temptations.

This is life.

This is how I know who I am!

This is the doorway to holiness, for without them there can be no humility, purification, or instruction in the ways of God.

To confront and conquer the trials and tribulations of life is to grow in endurance, patience, peace, trust, fervent prayer, and spiritual advancement.

O Lord, grant me the strength to recognize and conquer the trials, tribulations, and temptations of life.

O Lord, help me to know who I am!

Consecrated to You

O Lord, help me to consecrate my heart to Your heart.

Guide my judgments by Your wisdom, my actions by Your Spirit, my words by Your love, and my heart with a desire for heavenly wonders.

Free and liberate my soul from any distractions or unhealthy preoccupations.

Master my heart so that it may always ache for You and Your glory, that it may always worship the Father in spirit and truth.

Bless me with an undivided heart, a heart burning with love in times of prosperity as well as in times of poverty, in times of adversity as well as in times of calm, in times of trials and tribulations as well as in times of peace.

Loving You

In You, O Lord, I move and live and have my being.

In You my mind is enlightened, my actions directed, my heart lit on fire.

In my afflictions grant me the perspective of Your divine providence.

Bless me with the understanding, knowledge and wisdom

of seeing beyond this world's trials and tribulations.

Help me to realize that this world's difficulties are nothing when compared to living without You, O Lord.

May I grasp that the world's greatest suffering is nothing when compared to the suffering that is found in failing to love You.

In You, O Lord, I move and live and have my being.

In You my mind is enlightened, my actions directed, my heart lit on fire.

Accepting the Unavoidable

O Lord, teach me to accept that which is so hard to accept.

Aid me in accepting the disagreeable feelings that come from unfortunate situations and circumstances which do not correspond to my inclinations, needs or hopes.

Grant me the grace to embrace the unavoidable difficulties of life for love of You and the elevation of my soul.

Help me to understand that deep within the mystery of suffering is found a great treasure, the treasure of redemption and sanctification, of virtue and holiness.

Make me realize, as a Christian, that I possess the secret to accepting the sorrows of life.

The Little Daily Crosses

O Lord, help me to deal with the ordinary crosses of daily life.

Make me see in these daily crosses means of spiritual growth and progress.

While no great heroism is required in the carrying of these crosses, the gift of unreserved acceptance is a must.

These little crosses are little instruments geared toward sanctification, the elevation of virtues, and salvation.

These little crosses are transformed into spiritual gifts directed toward union with You:

They chip away and purify me of all that prevents me from being virtuous, from being God-like, from being in the image and likeness I was created to be like.

O Lord, prevent me from losing my serenity and confidence and help me to carry the crosses of day to day life with love and faith.

O Lord, clear away the scales before my eyes so that I may see that in every act of suffering there is concealed the mystery of redemption and sanctification.

O Lord Jesus, I gladly take up the crosses of everyday life because I know Your yoke is easy and Your burden is light.

By Love

It is by love that Christ transformed the Cross, an instrument of torture, into an instrument of salvation.

By imitating You, my Lord, unavoidable suffering finds a very important place in my life, a place that does not destroy my peace and serenity.

To be happy while experiencing pain! O what a mystery!

Grace me with that supernatural love that makes this a possibility!

Getting Up

O Lord, I feel so crushed.

Just as You fell into the ground on the road to Calvary, I so often feel that I too have been crushed into the ground.

May I share in Your pain when I am lonely, depressed, and ill.

May I feel the sting of the ground every time prayer seems dry and hard.

May I feel the tearing of my knees every time I experience darkness instead of faith, hope, and love.

O Lord, help me to fight the good fight in these times,

to get off the ground as You got off the ground.

Suffering in Resemblance of You

In suffering I assimilate myself to You, O Lord.

I seek to live Your life.

In my suffering I make up, by Your Will,

what is wanting in the sufferings of You, O Lord (Col. 1:24).

In my suffering I become a collaborator in the most

precious work of the salvation of souls;

I participate intimately in Your interior life and apostolic mission.

In my unavoidable suffering, in my love for You, I desire to be united with Your Passion, for to be united to Your Passion is to unite myself to Your intentions, to the glory of the Father and the salvation of souls.

In uniting myself to Your Passion I unite myself to the sanctification of suffering.

May I bear the unavoidable sufferings for You, in You, and with You so as to prolong Your Passion for the redemption and sanctification of souls.

May I be a Christ for others.

At Your Feet

I come to the foot of the Cross, O Lord, as Your student.

When I make myself the center of the universe, when I become preoccupied with material things, teach me to be at the foot of the Cross.

When my ego is out of place, when I am puffed up with pride, teach me to be at the foot of the Cross.

When my need to self-assert myself overtakes me, when lust, anger, gluttony, envy and sloth preoccupy my thoughts, teach me to be at the foot of the Cross.

At the foot of the Cross I will find humility, generosity, chastity, mildness, temperance, friendship, and diligence.

At Your feet mortify me so as to purify me, afflict me so as to heal me, embrace me so as to transform me.

Teach me, O Lord, to sit at the foot of the Cross, at Your feet.

From Cross to Glory

In the darkest and most painful of times, in the times when all seems lost, when all is reduced to defeat, when evil seems to have won, it is then that I must be at the foot of the cross with Mary, John, and Mary Magdalen.

It is then I must show my fidelity, my proof of authentic and unwavering love.

It is then that I must await the resurrection of this bruised, bloodied, pierced, disfigured, torn, lacerated, and wounded dead body.

And as I rejoice at the resurrection and the glorification of my Lord's body, may I rejoice in the little resurrections that daily occur in my own times of pain, defeat and loss, in my own times when my body seems bruised, bloodied, pierced, disfigured, torn, and lacerated.

Grant me, O Lord, the gift of transforming agony into glory.

In the darkest and most painful of times, may I sit at the foot of the cross and lay at the doorway of the sepulcher awaiting the resurrection.

O Lord, thank You for being my victory, my ransom, my salvation.

You Know Me, Lord

I hoped for strength that I might conquer the world:

I was given humility so that I might conquer myself.

I hoped for great health that I could evangelize the world;

I was given infirmity that I might evangelize a person in need.

I hoped for riches that I might feel secure;

I was given poverty so that I might be wise and dependent on You.

I hoped for power that I might control things according to my desires;

I was given weakness so that Your desires might control and guide me.

I hoped for honor, so that I could influence the world;

I was given dishonor so that I could quietly and anonymously serve You with the greatest joy.

I got very little that I ever hoped for, but everything that I ever could have desired.

Almost despite myself, You gave me light, happiness, and peace.

O Precious One, thank You for knowing me more than I know myself.

The Purifying Night

O Lord, in my trials and tribulations help me to see a means of rooting out my imperfections.

Root out my pride and egoism, from whence comes all imperfections.

In my lack of sensible consolation, detach me from all that is contrary to Your honor and glory and transform my being into a new being.

Help me walk through this dark night where emptiness abounds, where affections and feelings seem extinguished, where all is dry.

O Lord, in my difficulties help me to be well disposed in order to see a means of rooting out my imperfections so as to enter into the realm of Goodness, Purity and Infinite Beauty, the realm of You, My Lord.

Grant Me Light

O Lord, take away the blindness and groping in the dark that finds no meaning in suffering.

Grant me the grace to know that Your Ways are beyond my ways.

Give me, O Lord, the supernatural senses to see events in Your light, to penetrate the mystery of suffering and uncover a glimpse into its meaning.

Faith, Hope, and Love

O God, grant me the gifts of faith, hope, and love.

O God, grant me the gift of faith.

In faith You perfect and transcend my reasoning and understanding. You free me from egoism, passions, jealousies, whims, and all those things which hinder my inner call of grace. You free me to bear fruits of devotion and confidence and a certitude and firmness in actions. You enable me to penetrate the deepest mysteries of divine revelation. You enable me to act promptly to decisions regarding my eternal destiny. Error is easily identified and all that is not of You screams emptiness.

O God, grant me the gift of hope.

In hope You help me to persevere and overcome the difficulties of life. In hope I am purified to love You sincerely, to walk into the unknown with a sense of certitude, trust, abandonment, firmness and direction toward that which is the hope of all. You become all that is hoped for, my end, my happiness. In hope You polish off the lingering defects of presumption and discouragement.

You help me overcome an overemphasis on Your mercy and an under-emphasis on Your justice, an overemphasis on Your gift of pardon and an under-emphasis on repentance, an overemphasis on the assurance of salvation and an under-emphasis on confidence.

O God, grant me the gift of love.

In love I find the resemblance of You. In love I conquer sin and its inclinations. I conquer the distorted desire for pleasures, honors, fame, wealth and anything that is not properly ordered to Your will. I conquer my self-centeredness and seek to make the love of God and neighbor one living reality. In love I love You, O God, for simply being You, and not for what I can get from You. In love I love my neighbor for being in the image and likeness of You and not for what he or she can give me. In love I unite my will with Yours in imitation of Your Son uniting his human will with his divine will. In love I encounter the mystery of suffering and in suffering I encounter the mystery of love. In love I can do all things. In love I am *divinized*, glorified.

O God, grant me the gifts of faith, hope, and love. Grant me that desire to love You, to think of You, to adore You, to pray to You, to thank You, to ask pardon of You, and to aspire to You.

Transfigured

O Lord of Mount Tabor, transfigure me.

O Lord, cure me, heal me, and encourage me.

Teach me to turn to the right, to follow You, to contemplate You and offer myself entirely to You, to Your disposal.

Mold me, break me, transform me,
until I am transfigured and glorified.
O Lord of Mount Tabor, transfigure me.

World's Approval

The worldly seek the approval of all.
The holy seek the approval of You, O Lord, and only You.
The world and all that is in it passes away.
The world is empty and those who seek the things of the world are even more empty.
Blessed Mother, teach me to see the emptiness of the world and to cherish the approval of your Son.
What more do I need, O Lord, than to bask in Your love for me and my love for You.
May You be to me what You were to Your Mother: all in all.

The Beatitudes

O Gentle Lord, grant me the gift of the beatitudes.
When I am "poor in spirit" I grow in confidence, humility, and dependence upon You.
When I am "mournful" I find Your consolation and comfort.
When I am "meek" I recognize my place within Your kingdom.
When I "hunger and thirst for righteousness" I grow in Your will and in submission to Your will for all.
When I am "merciful" I grow in authentic justice,
for justice without mercy is nothing but cruelty.
When I am "pure of heart" I am always in Your presence.

When I am a "peacemaker" I grow and promote peace in my heart and in the hearts of others with a gentle, docile spirit ordered to Your providential plan.

When I am unjustly "persecuted" I grow in strength to know and fight for justice at whatever cost to me.

O Precious Lord, grant me the gift of the beatitudes so that I might find sincere happiness, for where real happiness is found, You are there!

O Gentle Jesus, Your beatitudes express my innermost desire for happiness, my innermost hunger for You, "happiness itself."

Father

O Lord, You experienced all things I experience with the exception of sin, and for this reason, You know more than all what I truly need to be fully, sincerely and authentically human.

When I cry, "abba," "Father," teach me what communion, Church, Trinity, and being created in Your image and likeness are all about.

Teach me straightforward simplicity, filial trust, Your assurance, humble boldness, and the certainty of being loved.

When I cry, "who art in heaven," help me to recognize Your majesty and presence in my heart and in the heart of the just.

Help to recognize Your house, my true homeland to which I am heading and to which, mysteriously, I already belong.

When I cry, "hallowed be Thy name," may I recognize Your holiness, preciousness, and majesty.

May I recognize that You are worthy of all praise and thanksgiving.

When I cry, "Thy kingdom Come," entrust me with the power to bring about the fulfillment of Your kingdom, a kingdom of love.

When I cry, "Thy will be done on earth as it is in heaven," make me realize that all are called to be saved and come to the truth, that all are called to love one another, that all are called to do all in accordance with Your will, that all are called to imitate You, the Son, in the example of obedience to the Father.

When I cry, "give us this day our daily bread" help me to realize Your infinite goodness, Your desire for solidarity Your call to trust and surrender, Your call to meet in responsibility and justice the material and spiritual needs of Your people, and Your command to be nourished by Your Body, Blood, Soul, and Divinity.

When I cry, "and forgive us our trespasses as we forgive those who trespass against us" I am reminded that the love of God and the love of neighbor are one inseparable reality.

When I cry, "and lead us not into temptation" give me Your strength to be set free from the snares of evil.

Grant me the ability to determine between temptations, trials and tribulations, which are for my personal growth and those which lead to sin and death.

Help me to persevere and unmask the lies behind the temptations of life and to become strong in You.

When I cry, "deliver us from evil" I am asking for Your protection against the cunning and wiles of the devil.

I am asking for the gift, the ability to unmask the evil which parades as good.

Our Father, who art in heaven, empower me with the fullness of the Gospel mystery so that I may win the crown of victory, win the spiritual battle.

Eternal Life

Christ, you are the morning star who came back from the dead.

You entered death to destroy its sting, to be its savior, its redeemer, to release the righteous and free the just.

From Abraham's bosom you brought the righteous into the vision of God.

You preached the words of eternal life.

You completed the task of spreading your redemptive work to all peoples of all times and places.

Jesus, Author of Life, by dying you destroyed the sting of death.

Jesus, holder of the 'keys of death' you delivered me from my fears of death.

Arise, You say, for you are the life of the dead!

Have Mercy

Lord, have mercy.

Christ, have mercy.

Lord, have mercy.

Lord Jesus, Son of God, have mercy on me a sinner.

II

In Imitation of Mary's Heart

"Anyone who has inwardly accepted suffering becomes more mature and more understanding of others, becomes more human."

Joseph Cardinal Ratzinger
His Holiness Pope Benedict XVI

Mold me, Mary

O beautiful mold of Mary, where Jesus was naturally and divinely formed, pray for me.

Mary, you molded your Son, Jesus, God and man.

May I be broken down and melted so that I may be poured into your mold.

May you mold me in such a way that I might appear as your Son.

Mold me to be fully human so that I may participate in the divinity of your Son.

O beautiful mold of Mary, where Jesus was naturally and divinely formed, pray for me.

Intense Love

Blessed Mother, as you carried your Savior you were gifted with intense love.

As Jesus was within your womb, may He be within my heart so that I too may have an intense love for God and His people.

As Jesus was united so closely to you, may He be united to me.

Help me realize that in this intimate relationship, You, Heavenly Father, love in me what you see and love in your Son, Jesus.

Blessed Mother, may your sentiments toward your Son be my sentiments.

Blessed Mother, as you carried your Savior, you were gifted with intense love.

May I be gifted with such love!

Dear Mary

Mary, my refuge and counselor, guide me in my times of dryness and even coldness.

When I fail to feel the tender love and the sensible sweetness of your Son's presence, guide me.

Help me to imitate your humility, your *fiat*, your fervent heart, especially in times where the problems of life seem so overwhelming.

Mary, my refuge and counselor, help me to put all under the submission of your Son's divine providence for me.

Mother of Pure Love

Mary, intercede for me so that I may have the fervor of the saints,

the zeal of the martyrs,

the purity of the confessors,

the faith and open hearted-ness of children,

and the virtues of the holy virgins.

May I be blessed with a new heart that is ardent and generous, tender and compassionate.

And at the end of my life, help me to find within that last breath the honor and glory of a life lived with your Son.

Help me, Mary

O Precious Mother Mary, comfort me from the foot of the Cross when I, like your Son, feel condemned or even crucified for simply being dedicated to a life of faith.

When I cannot understand the hate of others, help me, Mary, to follow your example of trust and compassion.

When I cannot understand those who have turned their backs on me after all I have done for them, help me, Mary, to follow your example of faith and forgiveness.

When I give unconditional love and am responded to with "crucify him," may I follow your example, Mary, and find assurance in your Son.

Mary, O Precious Mother Mary, comfort me from the foot of the Cross.

O Mary Most Holy

O Mary, my hope, in times of pain may I imitate your serenity,

in times of anguish your tranquility,

in times of distress your poise,

in times of misery your composure,

in times of agony your peace,

in times of torment your calm.

O Mary, my hope, in times of affliction may I imitate your self-assurance.

Grant me, through your Son, an ability to forget the unfortunate circumstances of my past, an ardent fidelity to living a holy life in this present state, and an eager belief in my future salvation.

Humble and Prudent

Dear Mary, help me to be prudent and humble.

When life seems so overwhelming,

when I want to lash out,

grant me prudence to react as you would want me to react,

to be humble, so that I may know myself the way I truly am and to seek out your Son's help as I truly need it.

Dear Mary, help me to be prudent and humble.

Imitate Mary

If the blessed apostle Paul reminded the faithful to imitate him as he imitated Christ, how much more should we imitate Mary   (1 Cor. 4:16)?

In imitating you, O Blessed Mother, I imitate your Son.

Help me to be faithful, loving, hopeful, peaceful, obedient, humble, pure, zealous, generous and other-centered.

Help me, O Queen of Virtues, to be blessed with the same virtues that made you so able to deal with the sorrows of life.

Help me, O Masterpiece of Grace, to respond as you did to the graces of your Son in good times and bad.

Bless me, Blessed Mother, to see beyond the sufferings of the journey, to the victory of the Cross.

Bless me, Master of Christians, to transform my suffering into a redemptive work, a sharing in your Son's work of redemption   (cf. Col. 1:24).

O Mother of the Church, teach me to put before me, above all, the life of grace.

Mary, Star of Light

Dear Mary, intercede for me so that I may see, as your Son wills, life in the fullness of grace that you saw it.

When evil and darkness disguise themselves as angels of light,

when the spirit of falsehood disguises itself as the spirit of truth, grant me the light to see through the deceptions of the devil.

Dear Mary, help me to overcome the mirages of life which seek to destroy my being.

Dear Mary, intercede for me so that I may see as you see, through the gift of a rightful obedience of faith.

Keep Me Pure

O Virgin of Virgins, help me to be pure and spotless in my life, for so much suffering is tied to my sins.

O Virgin Most Pure, help me to cope with the sins I have

inflicted upon the world and the sins the world has inflicted upon me!

Help me to watch over my heart, to keep it pure, so as to be watchful of those who seek to misuse my natural weaknesses to bring about my fall into misery.

Blessed Mother, I have enemies within and enemies outside and all around, pray that the grace within this earthen vessel may not be snatched away in times of sadness.

May I never be presumptuous;

May I always guard the treasure of grace within me,

for it is then that I will find the ability to cope with all that surrounds me.

It is then that your Son will dwell in my soul, enlightening it, supporting it, and rewarding it with eternity.

It is then that I will find the victory of my life!

Obedience of Faith

Mary, Mother of God, you have taught me what it means to have an obedience of faith.

You have taught me that all that is contrary to the pillar and bulwark of truth, the Church, is to be avoided.

May I live my faith in the spirit you lived your faith, dearest Mother of Mothers.

In times when the mystery of faith is far beyond my comprehension, help me to walk as you walked into the mystery with assurance, without doubt, and with a mind in obedience to faith and God's loving guidance, a mind with the spirit of the Church.

Help me, dearest Mother, to believe what eye cannot see

and reason cannot fully comprehend.

Help me to judge reality not through my own selfish being, but through the light of faith.

Sword of Sorrow

O Mary, Queen of Martyrs, it was prophesied that you would be pierced with a sword of sorrow.

In my sadness, my tears and sighs, grant me submissive peace, the peace of knowing that all is part of God's divine plan, that nothing is by chance or coincidence.

Aid me in seeing what your Son wants me to see, what He wants me to learn.

Grant me the understanding that within the mystery of suffering is the mystery of love and within the mystery of love is the mystery of suffering.

May I see all, the good times and the difficult times, as moments of grace, as moments of growth and purification, as moments of salvation.

May I see that your Son will never allow me to be pushed, tempted, tested or tormented beyond my strength.

Yes, He may push me to the very edge of the cliff, but He shall never allow me to fall as long as I hold unto Him.

O Mary, Queen of Martyrs, it was prophesied that You would be pierced with a sword of sorrow.

Sacred Heart of Mary

O Sacred Heart of Mary, bless me with a heart like yours, a heart burning with love, the love of God.

Help me realize that a heart that is separated in any way from your Son's is a heart that can never overcome the emptiness and afflictions of life.

May I give my heart, my freedom, and my very self to the Sacred Heart of your Son, a heart whose blood floods me with the abundant graces of salvation.

O Sacred Heart of Mary, whose heart was pierced at the foot of the Cross, help me to bear the unbearable, to overcome the pains and distresses in life.

O Mother Most Merciful

O Mother Most Merciful, through your intercession grant me the gift to realize that the things of this world are temporary and never sufficiently fulfilling.

In my times of misery or torment, help me to see that this world is passing and the world to come is all that really counts.

O Mother Most Merciful, may your Son grant me a heart preoccupied with the things of heaven rather than the things of the world, with the glory and honor of the building up of the kingdom, and for the triumph of God's will.

O Mary, Most Holy, help me to overcome the pains, distresses, miseries, agonies, torments, and afflictions of life the way you did!

Help me to imitate you in alleviating sorrow, calming fears, dissipating doubts, and the wisdom to act wisely for the good of my soul and the souls of others.

Crown of Immortality

O Blessed Mother, if I were to die today would I be prepared?

O Mary, Refuge of the Needy, intercede for me, now and at the hour of my death.

What good is it if I have all the riches, honors, esteem, and praise the world can shower me with when faced with my eternal destiny, my immortality.

What good is it to have gained the whole world, which disappears upon death, only to lose my soul?

O Mary, Refuge of the Needy, make me appreciate that life without your Son is not life at all.

O Blessed Mother, Protector of Vocations, intercede for me so that my last end, my eternal destiny may be one overflowing with the fruits of grace-filled works and the eternal sigh of love.

Dormition

When You, O Lord, were laying the foundations of the world, the Blessed Mother, was in Your plans and intentions.

You, Blessed Mother, were in your Son's plans as the refuge of sinners, the support of the just, the hope of the afflicted, the comfort of the inconsolable, and the pattern of our eternal destiny.

You, Blessed Mother, were in your Son's plans as the spouse of the Spirit who would usher in an age of comfort amidst affliction, counsel amidst doubt, strength amidst trials, and guidance amidst confusions.

You, Blessed Mother, were in your Son's plans to show us a glimpse of heaven in the mystery of your dormition by pointing to a place where pleasure exists without pain, where joy exists without anxiety, where rest exists without disquietude, where peace exists without fear, and where enjoyment exists without boredom.

When You, O Lord, were laying the foundations of the world, the Blessed Mother was in Your plans and intentions.

Blessed Mother, pattern of my life, grant me the rest that makes up for all weariness and the consolation that outweighs all suffering.

May I Too

O Mary, may I too cry out with joy,
"O God You are mighty and have done great things for me."

O Mary, may I too cry out with joy that "I am the servant of the Lord."

In your humility and sincere modesty, may I too only think of God and His mercy, wisdom, power, goodness, and what His gifts have done for me in the past and will continue to do for me now and at the end of my life.

O Mary, may I cry out to you, now and at the hour of my death.

Down from the Cross

O Lord, I have experienced defeat.

I have been taken down from the cross, with all my strength exhausted.

I settle now in your arms, Mary, for you are my Mother.

Take care of me;

anoint me with your tears.

Embrace and comfort me as you once embraced and comforted your Son.

Mary, My Love

Mary, my love, may my love for you rise like incense into your presence.

May I imitate you in offering up my pierced heart, my struggles and pains.

May I, like you, Mother Mary, never forget the redemptive value of suffering.

Continue to teach me, through your intercessory prayers and example, how to imitate you and make my life a share in the redemptive sufferings of your Son.

Mary, Most Humble

O Mary Most Humble, you conceived the Savior in your humility.

Teach me to be humble, to know myself as your Son sees and knows me, for it is then that I know who I truly am.

Cleanse away the pride that stains, enslaves, and distorts the core of my very being.

May I understand that "whoever humbles himself shall be exalted."

Make me among the least so I may dwell among the great.

O Mary Most Humble, grant me through your intercessions a humble heart, a heart that chases after God's, a heart open to the mysteries of the spiritual life.

Teach me to recognize my weaknesses and to depend on God, the only source of my greatness and glory.

O Mary Most Humble, teach me to see that only by the means of a humble heart will I be able to find peace, happiness, and light.

Mary, Queen of Humility

Dear Mary, why do I seek the respect of humans, sometimes at great costs?

Why do I allow myself to fall and be manipulated all in the name of pride and ambition?

What good are the world's illusionary and empty honors?

What good does envy or jealousy bring?

What good does living for the here and now, for the things of this world truly give me?

Humility, the doorway to holiness, is what I really want?

For, more than anything in this transitory world, I want to hear the only thing that will ultimately mean anything: "In you my child I find my delight."

Mary's Heart

O Lord, bless me with Mary's heart, a heart that pulsates in union with Your heart.

Help me, O Lord, through a heart like Your Mother's to find help in need,

comfort in affliction,

light amidst darkness,

counsel in making difficult decisions,

guidance in confusion,

good example during secular times,

edification in times of ignorance,

and fervor in carrying out Your mandates.

O Lord, bless me with Mary's heart, a pierced heart pulsating for You.

Mary's Sacred Heart

Mary, show me the thoughts and feelings that are hidden within your sacred heart.

Write upon my heart what is upon your heart.

Give me a heart like yours, filled with the fire of holy love.

Mary of the Infant Jesus

Mary, Mother of the infant Jesus, grant me a spirit of authentic love.

In the stable of Bethlehem, Jesus was born.

You were rejected, refused, and even scornfully turned away from lodgings.

How lonely it must have felt?

How abandoned you and Joseph must have been during the severe, cold weather?

Yet you were in peace and filled with the spirit of love as you gave birth to the infant Savior amidst His creatures and His shepherds.

In among the poorest of the poor, you, O blessed Mother, found the treasure of all treasures.

Deprived of much, you found all!

In your Arms, Mary

O Lord, I have experienced defeat.

I have been taken down from the cross, with all my strength gone.

I have "fought the good fight."

I settle now in your Mother's arms, for she is my Mother too.

May she take care of me and anoint me with her tears.

O Lord, may her embrace give me comfort.

Hands of Mary

Hands of Mary, dry my tears,
caress my face,
protect me from the forces of evil.
Take me to your Son here and at the end of my life.
Support me in serving God,
comfort me in my suffering.
Show me the way to your Son.
Care for me as you cared for your Son, and always be there for me.
Grant me the gift of your Son, and the virtues and graces of your Son.
Keep me away from the proud and powerful and direct me to the wise and humble.
Hands of Mary, keep me away from all that is not for the honor and glory of your Son.

Safe Harbor

Holy Mary, Mother of God, pray for me now and at the hour of my death.
Holy Mary, Star of the Sea, lead me to a safe harbor.
When death should come, Blessed Mother, take me into your embrace, bring me to your Son and implore Him to accept me into His Kingdom.
O Precious Mother, in your embrace I will find salvation, for your Son will surely not refuse you, for he has never refused you.
Holy Mary, Mother of God, pray for me now and at the hour of my death.
Holy Mary, Star of the Sea, lead me to a safe harbor.

Seven Sorrows of Mary

O Mary of great sorrows, pray for me.

I

Simeon reminded you, O Blessed Mother, that a sword would pierce your heart at the foot of the Cross.

Comfort me, Mary, when my heart is pierced by the sorrows of life.

II

As you, Mary and Joseph, fled into Egypt how heavy must have been the sorrow of knowing that your son was rejected, unwanted and even threatened with death.

Comfort me, Mary, when I feel rejected, unwanted, and even when people could care little about my life.

III

O how painful must have been the loss of your Son!

O what thoughts must have rushed through your mind as you sought to find your Savior, your Son.

Help me, in times of panic, to find where the source of my meaning, purpose, light, happiness, and peace are to be found.

IV

O how your heart must have anguished at seeing your Son tortured and mocked.

When life tortures me and even mocks me in times of pain, anguish, distress, misery, agony, torment, and affliction help me to find comfort in the sharing in your Son's mission of redemption.

V

As you, Mary, stood under the Cross and watched your son suffer and die, how piercing the pain must have been to know that you could do nothing to relieve the pain.

In those times when the pain of life is unbearable, when it is beyond my capacity to deal with, renew me with the breath of life and the recognition that after the cross comes the resurrection, the victory.

VI

How heavy your heart must have been Mary to be cradling your dead Son in your arms.

O how potent must have been your anguish and tears.

O Mary, when all seems lost, when all seems empty, hopeless, and without hope, may I run into your embrace for consolation.

VII

My Son is now in the sepulcher, behind a rock.

How deep must have been your sadness?

In times of loneliness, of sorrow, remorse, gloom, rejection, uncertainty, confusion, ambivalence, and discouragement, give me the gift, O Lord, to persevere till the third day, the day of renewal and rejuvenation.

O Mary of great sorrows, pray for me.

Hail Mary

When I pray, "Hail Mary, full of grace," may I seek to live a life filled with grace.

When I pray, "The Lord is with you," may the Lord be with me and protect my soul.

When I pray, "Blessed are you among women," may I recognize that all those who are with your Son are blessed beyond imagination.

When I pray, "Blessed is the fruit of thy womb," may I realize that within me is the presence of your Son's image and likeness, that within me is the temple of God.

Holy Mary, Mother of God, pray for me, now, and at the hour of my death.

Mother, most kind, stand by me!

III

Conclusion

"Now I rejoice in my sufferings for your sake, and in my flesh I complete what is lacking in Christ's afflictions for the sake of his body, that is, the Church" (RSV, Col. 1:24).

"Problems just do arise. Certain decisions, failures, human inadequacies, disappointments, all these get to us—and indeed should get to us. Problems are meant in fact to teach us to work through things like that. If we became steel-hard, impenetrable, that would mean a loss of humanity and sensibility in dealing with other people. Seneca the stoic said: Sympathy is abhorrent. If, on the other hand, we look at Christ, he is all sympathy, and that makes him precious to us. Being sympathetic, being vulnerable, is part of being a Christian. One must learn to accept injuries, to live with wounds, and in the end to find therein a deeper healing" (God and World, Ignatius, 21-22).

Joseph Cardinal Ratzinger
His Holiness Pope Benedict XVI

"Now I rejoice in my sufferings for your sake, and in my flesh I complete what is lacking in Christ's afflictions for the sake of his body, that is, the Church" (RSV, Col. 1:24).